50 GOLDEN NUGGETS

LASER SHARP QUOTES DESIGNED TO SHAPE YOUR DAY

ALISA BELL

authorHOUSE®

AuthorHouse™
1663 Liberty Drive
Bloomington, IN 47403
www.authorhouse.com
Phone: 1 (800) 839-8640

Published by AuthorHouse 10/10/2016

ISBN: 978-1-5246-4312-6 (sc)
ISBN: 978-1-5246-4311-9 (e)

Print information available on the last page.

Any people depicted in stock imagery provided by Thinkstock are models, and such images are being used for illustrative purposes only. Certain stock imagery © Thinkstock.

This book is printed on acid-free paper.

DEDICATION

This book is dedicated to my dear friend Chris Hughes, who pushed me, supported me and encouraged me in every dream I ever expressed.

To my dear friend, and Editor, Erica Walker. Your precise eye and attention to detail is priceless.

To all of my clients, because of you I am the Master Life Strategist that I am today. Thank you!

To my Parents, friends, and loved ones, thank you for your prayers and support.

FOREWORD

I used to wonder why emotional pain was allowed to enter our lives. It doesn't feel good, it makes you cry and worse, it dramatically lowers ones' self-esteem. I don't wonder anymore. I have a clearer understanding of emotional pain through personal experience. You see, emotional pain is the fertilizer that makes you strong. When people discount your value and worth, or underestimate your power, you have to make a choice to grow from the experience or live your life in a box of fear and doubt. Desiring the approval of man is the downfall of every successful person. Truly your approval should come from your higher power and then within. Anything else is just a bonus.

It is my heart's desire that this book makes you laugh, reflect and most importantly move forward with the vision of greatness that you possess inside.

Each quote is a nugget that begins with the letter "N" "Nugget". Just below it you will find the letters "BTN" "Behind the Nugget" It is a behind the scenes look at what inspired me to write the nuggets that you now hold in your hand. I also offer coaching wisdom to thrust you forward as you move through life. To the right of each page, I am asking you to journal your thoughts. What did the nugget make you feel? How does the nugget apply to your life or those close to you? It is important that you write it down because you may never have that thought again, and you will want to capture that heart moment to review later as this book is designed to be a tool to motivate you on a daily basis. You can focus on one nugget a day or read the entire book in one setting.

I hope you are inspired to dig a little deeper for a personal revelation. Growth is a journey in which we must actively participate. I'll leave you with this final thought; Life doesn't always warn us that hard times are coming. There are lessons that I never would have learned had I not gone through and overcome adversity. I'll share three very personal beliefs that keep me grounded: Love the pink Polar Bear, cherish the special safe, and finally, smell the roses, especially the purple ones.

To your success and happiness,

Coach Alisa

ABOUT THE AUTHOR

Alisa Bell is a nationally recognized Master Life Strategist, whose expertise lies in the field of coaching, specializing in emotional breakthrough coaching, as well as relationship coaching. Alisa is certified as a Christian Counselor through PCCCA, a Life Coach through the Coach Training Academy and a (DISC) Behavioral Consultant through CCI. Alisa is the mother of two amazing sons and currently resides in Dallas Ft Worth, Texas.

N...A kind word can warm the coldest heart and a gentle hand heals the pain.

BTN... In today's society it seems that people are so self-focused that they forget that others around them may be in pain. We are consumed with our issues, our bills and our successes. The person you greet on the street today may be contemplating a life changing decision. One smile from you may offer hope and a hand may restore their faith in mankind. Today I encourage you to smile at someone, and take note of whether or not they smile back. I guarantee you will feel better and chances are they will too.

Personal Reflections…

N... Love is something that is first caught and then nurtured.

BTN...I have heard story after story of people who fall in love. They all say, "I never saw it coming". "It just happened". "I wasn't even looking for love". That's because love has to be caught. You don't just decide to love the stranger you meet on the elevator, yet 5 years later and two children you are still together. Love evolves during times of bonding, sharing a meal, exchanging texts or lingering phone calls. Love is mystical for sure and it must be nurtured. Love grows when we feed it the elements that caused us to catch it in the first place. Check your love meter, is it time for a tune up?

Personal Reflections...

N... There is no truth sadder than the seer who won't see.

BTN... There are times that we are presented with abominable truths in our society and we choose to turn a blind eye or deaf ear. When main stream agendas are considered entertaining and not harmful, we are perpetuating the lie and in serious danger of having a hand in destroying a nation or worse a generation. What's happening in the world today that riles you up? What action can you take to bring change to that very thing? You can impact change with a letter to congress, a whispered prayer or even an organized event. You are a change agent, you have a voice.

Personal Reflections...

_____

_____

_____

_____

_____

_____

_____

_____

_____

_____

_____

_____

_____

_____

_____

_____

_____

_____

_____

_____

_____

_____

_____

_____

_____

_____

_____

_____

N... It is impossible to be fearless without first experiencing fear.

BTN... Fear is a giant magnified in our own minds. If you feed your fears, then like any organism that you feed, it will grow. If you starve your fears or better yet banish them, they will have no power over you. If you speak to the fear in your life and tell it "I'm going forward and you can't stop me" it will shrink and ultimately vanish. You will wake up happy and on fire and wondering why you didn't make a move sooner. Today is the day that you decide fear will not have rule over me. I choose to be brave, powerful and fearless. I choose to live out loud and not hide in the shadows anymore.

Personal Reflections...

N... Pursuing your vision for the future will lessen the pain of a troubled past.

BTN... Let's face it. We all have a past and we all have a story to tell. Some of those stories we might not want to tell. Maybe bad choices have made you feel disqualified in some way and you don't feel worthy of pursuing a dream that will lead to happiness. A bad choice should only serve as a reminder of what NOT to do again. Bad choices do not make you a bad person, they make you human. I want to encourage you to pursue that dream or vision. In doing so you will find validation of your worth and value. You are a good person capable of doing great things.

Personal Reflections…

_____

_____

_____

_____

_____

_____

_____

_____

_____

_____

_____

_____

_____

_____

_____

_____

_____

_____

_____

_____

_____

_____

_____

_____

_____

_____

_____

_____

_____

_____

N... Don't fear the unknown of higher heights, fear the safety and complacency of the ground.

BTN... The beauty of not knowing the greatness that lies ahead of you is this; the road before you has no footprints and you are carving out a path that is uniquely your own. Complacency will keep you stuck in the familiar and a resistance to move will keep you from seeing what's on the other side of the tunnel. There are many people who have pioneered paths to greatness by looking at the examples of others. Again no one has placed boots on the ground for your unique path; your road will have different bumps and turns. They have however left clues that you can follow. It's time to soar. Take flight and offer hope to those who are currently shaking in their boots. Be the example.

Personal Reflections…

N... Passion produces purpose and purpose produces results.

BTN... Going after a goal that you are not passionate about is the equivalent of watching wet paint dry. It has to happen but there is nothing exciting about it. It will produce results but it will not necessarily make you happy, it's just something that needs to be done. A goal that you are passionate about on the other hand, will make you skip, sing and do a little dance. You can't wait for the new morning to move onto the next steps in accomplishing your goal. You feel a sense of purpose and that will produce maximum results. When was the last time you were truly passionate about a project? On the next page I want you to write down the name of your passion project, set a start date and do it. The results will be simply amazing.

Personal Reflections...

N... The heart is the canvas that your destiny is written on.

BTN... Destiny is not some great idea that we came up with or that our parents wrote on a napkin before we were born. Our instructions and blueprint are written on the tablets of our hearts. So often we strain our brains trying to figure out next steps. "Who am I", and the proverbial "why am I here", when all we really need to do is tap into our hearts. Your heart contains everything you need to know about your future. You can sense when something is a right fit for you. Maybe you're stuck in a boring and unfulfilling job but it's keeping the lights on. Tap into your heart and find that dream. The resources will appear when you uncover the what. Now I'm not saying you should leave that bill paying job by any means! I am saying that if you power your dream it may become a new lucrative source.

Personal Reflections…

N... The success that I am in my mind inspires me to work hard every day.

BTN...I have a dream. Not just any dream mind you. It's big and colorful and probably defies the laws of gravity. It's also tucked away in my mind and only shared with my private vision board. You see everyone can't handle your dream. People may laugh, make fun of your dream and even lovingly discourage you. Does that sound like something you want in life? Of course not! So don't share it, build it and when it is fully ready to be presented to the world, they will see. What they thought was crazy, was actually genius in the making.

Personal Reflections…

N... You are the product of your thoughts. Power thoughts produce a powerful life.

BTN... If a man thinks he is great then he is. If a man thinks he is mediocre then he is. What you think about yourself is what others are going to think about you. Thoughts are free and unlimited. Are your creative thoughts in black and white or in Technicolor? Do your thoughts shock even you, they should. Your creative thoughts should be just wild enough to inspire you to do something outside of your normal personality. Who is that bold person waiting to be seen or heard? Present yourself in your best light. If you think it, you can become it.

Personal Reflections...

N... If I confess that I have arrived then my journey ends. Therefore I must press with all diligence and stay in the race.

BTN... The moment you feel that you've arrived and can sit down to enjoy the fruit of your accomplishments, is the same moment that you've decided that this is the beginning of the end. Don't misunderstand what I'm saying. Retirement is a wonderful gift that we all deserve after working hard. That however doesn't mean that we should stop being and doing in the earth. Become skilled in a hobby, travel, or mentor. Do something productive, DON"T kick back in the chair. Every day that you open your eyes is a gift. Share your gift, become the gift in someone else's life.

Personal Reflections...

N... Your future success does not have an expiration date.

BTN... Many times I set goals and give them a date. Often times I arrive at that date and my goal is not yet met. The good news is that it is within my power to simply change the date, not the goal. Maybe I just need a little more time, or money or resources. Personal goals are just that, PERSONAL. Change the date and keep it moving.

Personal Reflections…

_____

_____

_____

_____

_____

_____

_____

_____

_____

_____

_____

_____

_____

_____

_____

_____

_____

_____

_____

_____

_____

_____

_____

_____

_____

_____

N... Change is a small word with big impact.

BTN.... When you hear the word change what comes to mind? When I hear the word change I instantly think why? What I should think is; here's an opportunity for me to become better. Change should always be perceived as an opportunity for growth. Growth is good for the mind and soul. Not so much for the body if you're a fully mature adult.{Ahem} The point is, whatever mental image you conjure up regarding hearing the word change, change it. If it's negative, change it. If it's positive, still change it. Change the image you have of change and do something different. Remember this, good has the potential to become great and great has the potential to become phenomenal. True change begins with your words.

Personal Reflections...

N... Live your life by the expectations you've set for yourself and NOT the limitations of man.

BTN... Have you ever wanted to do something but somebody in your life said you can't do that? Did you listen? You may have and that's ok. There are people in our lives that we consider experts. Maybe it's our parents, mentors, teachers or friends. It could be anyone that you have given permission to speak into your life. Just remember that it's YOUR life. Wise counsel is good and encouraged, but ultimately it's your life and you should never allow anyone to put limitations on your ability. Graciously listen to trusted advisors and apply all that is good and useful. Let the counsel of others add to your ultimate decision, just don't let it become the deciding factor.

Personal Reflections…

_____

_____

_____

_____

_____

_____

_____

_____

_____

_____

_____

_____

_____

_____

_____

_____

_____

_____

_____

_____

_____

_____

_____

_____

_____

N... Critique the flaws you THINK you see in me today, for tomorrow you will have to look a little higher to do it again.

BTN... Self-examination is not only needed in the life of an individual but required. When someone points out what they perceive as my flaws I thank them. Notice I said I THANK them, not agree with them. You see they just gave me a reason to examine myself. First I look deep to see if it is a flaw or a unique asset. I then search to see if my delivery or approach could be tweaked. When all of this is done, I emerge as a stronger, wiser person. Thank your haters because they are only making you better.

Personal Reflections…

N... Vision is birthed in the atmosphere where faith is welcomed.

BTN... If you don't believe in your vision surely no one else will. If you don't have faith to believe that the vision will come to pass, it will end up on the altar of hopelessness. It costs nothing to believe. You can begin by believing that your belief will be inspired. Challenge yourself to starve your doubts and breathe new life into your situations. Faith is an invisible force with great power. Faith must be invited by the visionary. We all have a measure of faith, but did you know that your faith can be increased just by asking? Imagine if you had more faith to help you believe that the vision will come to pass. The possibilities are endless.

Personal Reflections…

N... Allow fear to be your greatest motivator. Give yourself permission to do the thing that your inner self says can't be done. After you do it, serve notice to that inner voice called fear and serve it walking papers. You are amazing! You can do anything!

BTN... Fear has a very paralyzing affect on most people. Where does fear come from? It comes from within. So the powerful coaching question I want to ask right now, is why are you allowing something as toxic as fear to be in your personal space? Is it serving you? Is it stopping you? Is it deserving of a place in your mind? When you answer these questions you will disarm the power of fear and its grip on your life. Fear happens to all of us at unforeseen times in our life. When it happens recognize it and make a conscious choice to evict it immediately. Replace that negative with a positive. I choose not to fear because _____!

Personal Reflections…

N...A leader is only as great as their willingness to serve. The leader who serves much leads well.

BTN...I have sat under some great leaders in my lifetime and I plan to sit under many more. Do you know how I arrived at that seat? I served. I cleaned snow off of cars in the winter for the leader I wanted to have a conversation with. I cooked meals for the leader that I wanted to have a conversation with. I bought coffee, lunch or dinner for the leader I wanted to have a conversation with. I SERVED and I walked in humility. Volunteer is not a dirty word. It may be the key to your next seat at the table.

Personal Reflections…

N... True winners have winning thoughts before they ever take the prize. See yourself winning.

BTN... In my mind....there's always a party going on. I see myself as the best in my field, I see the top awards in my hands, and I see the audience that I want to motivate. You have to visualize the success that you want to achieve. If it exists then you should be able to see it in your mind. If it doesn't exist then you can create it. Our imaginations are so powerful. They allow us to dream and create scenarios that others can't fathom. The only thing missing from your big dream is YOU! When you see it in your mind's eye make sure you put yourself in the vision. Don't just see the prize, see yourself holding the prize.

Personal Reflections…

_____
_____
_____
_____
_____
_____
_____
_____
_____
_____
_____
_____
_____
_____
_____
_____
_____
_____
_____
_____
_____
_____
_____
_____
_____
_____
_____

N... It's never too late to fall in love, and if you've never been in love, you should try it at least once.

BTN... Love is a very scary thing. It's a feeling that cannot be described the same by the two people in it. Love is suffocating and exhilarating, a rush like no other. Love washes over you like a wave and you can't wait to catch the next one. Love is an ocean that you never want to leave. Ultimately love is an experience that we should cherish and give a special place in our hearts.

Personal Reflections…

N... Your present struggle is the road map to your greatest success.

BTN... The frustration that you currently feel should be turned into creative energy. What are you struggling with? Failed relationship, job loss, weight issues? You can sit and wallow in all of those issues or you can do something about it. Instead of sitting there thinking about what is, think about what will be and then execute!

Personal Reflections…

N... My future is bright for I see my reflection in the stars.

BTN... When life feels overwhelming to me, I go outside and try to count the stars. There are times that I don't see a single star in the sky so I wait. What I discovered in my time of waiting for the stars to appear is that dark clouds were covering them. Sounds like life right? So now I wait patiently for the dark clouds to pass and they do pass. When that happens I find that the stars are too many to count. Stars represent opportunities; there are many just waiting for you to pick one. Why not pick the biggest and brightest one and see your reflection in it.

Personal Reflections...

N... Become skilled at encouraging yourself. You are your biggest cheerleader, and no one wants success for you more than you.

BTN... When we become discouraged in life, it's hard to motivate ourselves to move forward. There's no band, no pep squad and no rocket to ride. You have to creatively step outside of yourself and find that motivation. If you're not your own life coach then hire one (hint, hint), read a book about self-motivation or listen to motivational speakers online. Soon you will gain the tools to motivate yourself. Then and only then will you become the best version of you that you were always meant to be.

Personal Reflections...

N... Destroy the weed at the root and it won't be able to destroy your crop.

BTN... So often we treat symptoms that our problems present rather than going after the original source of the problem. Before you know it that symptom grows and creates a new problem. Stop what you're doing and tackle the problem right away. This way there is no need to treat symptoms.

Personal Reflections...

_____

_____

_____

_____

_____

_____

_____

_____

_____

_____

_____

_____

_____

_____

_____

_____

_____

_____

_____

_____

_____

_____

_____

_____

_____

_____

_____

_____

N... The best romantic relationships begin with friendships. You share your best moments with your friends, so love is an easy add.

BTN...I once told a man that I wanted to be his best friend, his everything. His response was pleasantly surprising. He said he had never been told that before. He held it close to his heart and I'm sure he always will. Our words carry great impact. Choose your words wisely and change the course of your destiny.

Personal Reflections…

N... Seed in the ground will turn it around. Patiently wait for your harvest for surely it will come to pass.

BTN... Have you ever heard the saying "A watched pot never boils"? Have you ever tested that theory? Of course it will eventually boil but it seems to take longer when you're watching. If you go away and come back later you may find that the water has boiled lower than you wanted. Plant your seed of hope and go away. Enjoy the fruits of your last harvest, and before you know it a new one will spring up.

Personal Reflections…

N... Greatness is a privilege bestowed upon responsible men and women.

BTN... To be recognized as a great man or woman has everything to do with the character that you exhibit. It is not a position that you can assign to yourself. It has to be recognized in you and acknowledged by your peers. Walk in integrity not seeking fame or glory and greatness will be your portion.

Personal Reflections…

N... The grass on the other side is not necessarily greener than yours; a little fertilizer can do wonders to bring your lawn back to life.

BTN... Envying what someone else has is a waste of time. Is it someone else's marriage, lifestyle, or children that you envy? The time you spend watching them flourish is time that you could have been spending cultivating your own. Consider this, the ones that you're watching may be admiring you.

Personal Reflections…

N... Own your life's experiences, don't let them own you.

BTN... Life can come at us pretty hard sometimes. Things that you wish you could change or even worse, things you wish you hadn't done. The truth is that you did it or it happened. OWN IT! Grow from it! Consider it a lesson and glean the dos and don'ts to help guide your future.

Personal Reflections…

N... Evil desires torment great men and cause them to pursue the gates of hell.

BTN... People who choose to gain wealth through any means other than dedicated work and brain power are on the fast track to destruction. Illegal gain is temporary and will ultimately be taken from you.

Personal Reflections…

N... Adversity defines the strength of a man; peace defines the character of a man.

BTN... In life we will face many challenges and how we choose to deal with them will make or break us physically and emotionally. How do you rebound when a setback occurs? A small pebble in the road can trip a man and deter his course. That man now has to choose whether to pocket that pebble as a reminder of his determination to go on, or he can stand in place and stare at the pebble that kept him from moving forward. What are you doing with your pebbles?

Personal Reflections…

_____

_____

_____

_____

_____

_____

_____

_____

_____

_____

_____

_____

_____

_____

_____

_____

_____

_____

_____

_____

_____

_____

_____

_____

N... Personal vision can be likened to a clothes dryer. Occasionally you need to change the lint trap.

BTN... We sometimes get stuck on life's road to success. In an effort to get to the destination quicker we take detours, make changes and throw away those things that are useful but not necessary. Those useful things however are stuck in the lint trap of our lives. They didn't go anywhere; they are trapped in a different space of your brain. Clean the trap and make room for more of the unnecessary stuff to go. If you don't clean the lint trap, it won't work properly and neither will you.

Personal Reflections...

N... You know you have a bad attitude when you don't even want to spend time with yourself.

BTN... There are days that I choose not to answer the phone, because if the person on the other end knew how foul my mood was they would thank me for not taking their call. Can you relate? That being said, it would serve us well to adjust our attitudes and change the channel in our minds. Nothing good comes from bad, so why are we allowing ourselves to have a "bad" attitude? When you recognize a negative mood, take a walk, meditate, or watch mindless comedy for a while. Be intentional about feeling good.

Personal Reflections...

N... There is nothing as great as a man who honors a woman and her position in the earth.

BTN... Men want to feel appreciated by the woman they love, and women want to feel honored by the man they love. Women feel honored when the man takes the time to listen to her verbal and non-verbal cues. When a man masters the art of honoring his woman that man can conquer not only life but the world.

Personal Reflections…

N...A lifeline is only as good as the source it's plugged into.

BTN... You may be familiar with the TV show "Who Wants to be a Millionaire". There are several options for the contestants when they get stumped by a question. They can ask the audience, 50/50 or they can phone a friend. These are referred to as lifelines. I would imagine the contestant has a pretty clear idea of who they would choose as a lifeline if they get stuck. This person is probably wise, creative and most importantly, dependable. Do you have a lifeline? Have you considered the source? Write that person's name on the personal reflections page and list why they are your lifeline. If you don't have a name to add then you should evaluate the people in your inner circle.

Personal Reflections…

_____
_____
_____
_____
_____
_____
_____
_____
_____
_____
_____
_____
_____
_____
_____
_____
_____
_____
_____
_____
_____
_____
_____
_____
_____
_____
_____
_____
_____

N... There are no refunds on storybook fantasies, so live the life that you were predestined to live.

BTN... Everyone has a dream in their heart or at least they should. When we were children we dreamed of the ideal job, car, home, spouse, etc. These are fantasies, hopes or ambitions. There's nothing wrong with that, but we should always be rooted in reality. You may obtain a version of the fantasy but be very clear that modifications are fine and in most cases necessary. Build you future one brick at a time. Before you know it you will have the whole building.

Personal Reflections...

N... Pipe dreams are like coupons. You get half off or less and a short expiration date.

BTN... Write the vision and make it plain. A good man's steps are divinely directed. Instead of building the pipes that possibly lead to nowhere, build the stairs that lead to destiny and begin climbing.

Personal Reflections…

_____

_____

_____

_____

_____

_____

_____

_____

_____

_____

_____

_____

_____

_____

_____

_____

_____

_____

_____

_____

_____

_____

_____

_____

_____

_____

_____

_____

_____

N... Our creator does not follow us in our state of ignorance. He hands out wisdom in abundant supply.

BTN... Walking blindly through life is a waste of time. Wisdom is a commodity that is seldom used. Sadly people are in pursuit of worldly knowledge, book knowledge and even street knowledge. These types of pursuits take years to obtain and rarely provide the answers that one request for wisdom regarding one's life could simply and quickly answer. Give it a try...Ask.

Personal Reflections…

_____

_____

_____

_____

_____

_____

_____

_____

_____

_____

_____

_____

_____

_____

_____

_____

_____

_____

_____

_____

_____

_____

_____

_____

_____

_____

_____

N... If Mama is happy the family gets dessert; if Mama's not happy the family gets out!

BTN... You may have heard the saying "happy wife, happy life". Well I would like to expand on that concept. In this day and age, as sad as it may be, there is not always a husband in the house to keep the wife happy. Children who are well behaved and follow house rules will always get dessert. Why? Life then becomes easier for Mama. If Mama doesn't have to come home from work and scream about the dishes not being done, or the floors not being vacuumed, she can focus on baking for the darlings. If she has to scream, everyone can get out. Mama will then enjoy dessert alone.

Personal Reflections…

N... An eagle's eye is to be desired but a lazy man lacks focus and vision.

BTN... Eagles possess eyesight that is 4 to 8 times stronger than the average human. Eagles zoom in on the object they desire and strategically swoop in at the right time to possess said object. Eagles never lose focus. A lazy man who has no drive or sense of direction will never achieve his goals because he has probably not set them. He can't see the light at the end of the tunnel because his vision is limited. My advice to this man, start with a plan. What do you want to achieve? How much do you want to make? What is your skill set? When you answer these powerful questions your vision will become clear and the plan will take shape.

Personal Reflections…

_____

_____

_____

_____

_____

_____

_____

_____

_____

_____

_____

_____

_____

_____

_____

_____

_____

_____

_____

_____

_____

_____

_____

_____

_____

_____

_____

_____

N... Soar with eagles and you can cover the world, peck with chickens and you can cover the yard.

BTN... This one is pretty clear. Eagles can cover the expanse of the globe with a single thought of where they want to go. They have the capability to focus on the destination and arrive at a reasonably set time. Chickens however never leave the yard, unless they are headed to a bucket near you. They are waiting for the next batch of feed to arrive to satisfy their basic needs. Chickens have no ambition. It's just a matter of time before they are plucked! Don't be a chicken.

Personal Reflections...

_____

_____

_____

_____

_____

_____

_____

_____

_____

_____

_____

_____

_____

_____

_____

_____

_____

_____

_____

_____

_____

_____

_____

_____

_____

_____

_____

_____

N... Sleep is good for the natural man, rest is good for the spirit.

BTN... Sleep rejuvenates the body. It gives our minds a break from the daily grind and gives us strength to do it all over again. Rest on the other hand can be found at any time of the day or night. Rest is not about closing our eyes as much as it is about a peaceful state of mind. We must give ourselves permission to rest. Rest is not automatic, it must be desired. When you feel that you are at the end of your rope, put in a request for rest. It will change your life in ways you never imagined.

Personal Reflections...

N... You may have heard that nothing taste as good as thin, but I'll take a side of curves with that.

BTN... This one is for the ladies. There is nothing as attractive as a woman who is confident in her own skin. We're talking about a woman who is physically healthy, and who embraces her curves. A little roundness sets her apart from her male counterparts. Personally I have adopted the term "curvaceously thin". At the end of the day you should love the skin you're in. You should not try to modify your size by current beauty standards or the hot guy that you want to notice you. You are uniquely you and if you love yourself, others will love you just as you are.

Personal Reflections…

N... Painful memories are like walking on shattered glass, if a piece gets stuck, so do you.

BTN... Who knew a stroll down memory lane could last a lifetime? When you reflect on your past mistakes and failures you should look for the lessons to be gleaned, not the punishment that you think should be doled out. Forgive yourself and forgive the offender(s). If you practice this with every stroll you are less likely to get stuck.

Personal Reflections…

_____

_____

_____

_____

_____

_____

_____

_____

_____

_____

_____

_____

_____

_____

_____

_____

_____

_____

_____

_____

_____

_____

_____

_____

_____

_____

_____

_____

_____

N... Quiet moments are worth everything they cost you.

Peace is a rare commodity in the world today. Sometimes you just want to get away from yourself for a few hours let alone the spouse, the kids and the dog. I would encourage you to pay the price for momentary and long lasting peace. You may enjoy a golf outing, a spa day, or a trip to the beach. Whatever you find enjoyable that brings you peace and falls in line with your budget, do it. A little peace could result in a greater piece that life has to offer.

Personal Reflections…

_____
_____
_____
_____
_____
_____
_____
_____
_____
_____
_____
_____
_____
_____
_____
_____
_____
_____
_____
_____
_____
_____
_____
_____
_____
_____
_____
_____

N... Friendships are like vintage cars; they are reliable and get better with time.

BTN...A quality friendship is one of give and take. Granted there will be the one giving more than taking, but if you both agree to those terms then so be it. A good friend does not have set expectations of you but rather they accept you as you are. Friendships need to be nurtured and appreciated. If you haven't called your friend in a while, then take the time to do that today. Let them know how much you value who they are and what they mean to your life. That one gesture could make the difference in whether or not your friendship fades or grows.

Personal Reflections...

N…A woman behind the wheel of a car is a gift to all mankind.

BTN…Women are multi-talented behind the wheel of a car. When I was younger my mother would put on her lipstick, dig in her purse and blow my nose all before the light changed to green. Now I am not saying that women should do this while the car is in motion but I am saying that you can get quite a bit done while the red light is in play. Here's a thought, instead of applying lipstick try rehearsing your power thoughts and put a musical twist on them. I like me, I like my family, I like my job, I like my house, I like my life. Winning thoughts produce a winning day.

Personal Reflections…

N... Exercise is not only good for the body but it gives a boost to the mind and soul.

BTN... Exercise releases endorphins. Endorphins have been known to minimize pain and create euphoric feelings of peace and happiness. Therefore exercise has greater benefits than the exterior cosmetic boost that comes from looking good. Try exercising your mind using word puzzles or reading a good book. Stimulating the brain not only makes you smarter but also keeps you young.

Personal Reflections...

N... Apply tough love to your life's goals. Don't let yourself off the hook when it's time to grind.

BTN... There are times in our lives when we have to motivate ourselves to keep moving forward. Have you ever taken a break from a goal to celebrate a milestone on the way? That's great but you must be mindful of how long the celebration lasts. Enjoy the small victory but keep in mind that the journey is still ongoing. Do a happy dance, pat yourself on the back and get back in the race. The ultimate prize is only achieved when you cross the finish line. Don't settle for the honorable mention. Go for the gold.

Personal Reflections...

N... When life presents setbacks, it's not time to drawback. Start scripting your comeback and then take the stage! #TRUTH

BTN...I love the quote from the movie Forrest Gump "Life is like a box of chocolates". Everyday life is filled with challenges, surprises and mystery. Even the person with the most detailed plan can cite at least one thing during their day that didn't go according to their plan. When life throws a curve ball it can knock the wind out of us. It can take the song out of our hearts and it can leave us sitting on the side of the road dazed and confused. I want you to take the time to sit with your feelings. Yes this Coach is encouraging you to own those less than happy thoughts. It is only when you take the position of owning what has happened to you that you can begin to write the next chapter. Your next chapter will be greater than the loss that you experienced. How do I know that? You're still in the game, you haven't quit and failure is not an option. You are a winner and you will soon see that your best days are ahead of you and chocolate never tasted so good.

Personal Reflections…

Printed in the United States
By Bookmasters